WILD WEST

First published in Great Britain by
CAXTON EDITIONS
an imprint of
The Caxton Book Company,
16 Connaught Street,
Marble Arch, London, W2 2AF.

ISBN 1 84067 026 6

A copy of the CIP data for this book is available from the British Library upon request.

With grateful thanks to Helen Courtney

Created and produced for Caxton Editions by
FLAME TREE PUBLISHING,
a part of The Foundry Creative Media Company Ltd,
Crabtree Hall, Crabtree Lane,
Fulham, London, SW6 6TY.

Printed in Singapore by Star Standard Industries Pte. Ltd.

HEADStart

WILD WEST

*The History and Myths
of the American West
Explained in Glorious Colour*

MAUREEN HILL

CAXTON EDITIONS

❧ Contents ❧

Introduction 10

Moving the Border Westwards 12

Native American Peoples 14

Native American Peoples of the Plains 16

Mountain Men 18

Wagon Trains 20

Gold Fever 22

Ranches on the Plains 24

Cowboys 26

Homesteaders 28

The Pony Express 30

The Railroad 32

Ghost Towns 34

Justice in the Wild West 36

War Between the Settlers and the Native Americans 38

The Battle of Wounded Knee 40

Wild West Shows 42

Further Information and

    Picture Credits 44

Introduction

What do we mean when we talk about the Wild West? The West part seems simple – we are talking about the west of the United States of America. Some years ago 'the west' meant all the land on the west banks of the Mississippi River. The Wild part has many more meanings. Sometimes this refers to the people, mostly men, who lived there; sometimes 'wild' is used in connection with the land itself, which was uncultivated and untamed; 'wild' can also refer to the lack of law and order in the newly settled lands of Western North America.

Much of what we think about the Wild West comes from stories. First of all these stories were told in popular magazines and books, and later in films, particularly in the 1940s and 1950s. In the last century there were also travelling shows featuring people like Buffalo Bill Cody and Little Annie Oakley, who showed the world some of the skills and activities of the Western Cowboys. Some of these shows still exist today.

The period of the Wild West was quite a short one. It took less than a hundred years for the European settlers to explore, open up and finally settle the West. In that time the landscape and the lives of many Native American peoples were changed forever.

Moving the Border Westwards

In 1803 the boundary of the United States was the Mississippi River: only about a third of the area we know now as the USA. In that year President Thomas Jefferson bought a huge area in the centre of the continent from France. The United States paid $15 million for this area, called Louisiana by the French. This became known as the 'Louisiana Purchase'.

Jefferson was keen to increase the settled area of the USA. He sent explorers to find out what the land was like in Louisiana and beyond. In 1804 two men, Meriwether Lewis, Jefferson's own secretary, and William Clark, set off, with about 50 people, on a 28-month journey to reach the Pacific Ocean. They made reports on what the land was like, the soils, the minerals, the plants and especially the animals that could be trapped for fur.

Lewis and Clark, like many other early explorers of the West, were given a great deal of help by the Native American people. They taught

them how to survive on the Great Plains that covered the middle of America. It was from the Native Americans that the explorers learned much about the country they passed through.

The area of the USA almost doubled in size in a few short years in the 1840s. Texas, which had been a separate country and covered a large amount of land, joined the USA in 1845. The following year the area of Oregon was given to the USA by the British, who had previously claimed it. In 1848, following two brief wars with Mexico, the United States added California, New Mexico, Arizona and the Rio Grande River.

Native American Peoples

When Christopher Columbus first landed in the Americas – he did not actually land on the American mainland but on islands off the shore – he believed he was in the East Indies. Because of this he called the peoples he met 'Indians'.

The Native American peoples had followed their ways of life for thousands of years before the European settlers came. It is estimated that around five million people lived in the area now covered by the USA. It is also estimated that as many as three quarters of the Native American population were killed by European diseases. These diseases were new to the continent and the native peoples had no resistance to illnesses such as measles, smallpox and scarlet fever.

There were many different groups or 'tribes' of Native Americans, and their way of life depended on what sort of land they lived on. To the east of the Mississippi and to the south, near the Mexican border, they lived a settled life in villages built from huts, growing crops like maize. Indeed the Pilgrim Fathers, who are said to be the founders of the USA, would not have survived their first year in America without the help of the Algonquian tribe.

In most tribes, the women did the majority of the day-to-day work such as cooking, looking after the children, growing crops and preparing animal skins to make into clothing, bags or bedding. The men spent their time hunting and fishing for food. Occasionally they fought against other tribes.

Native American Peoples of the Plains

On the Great Plains to the west of the Mississippi, the tribes were 'nomadic', they moved around in communities across the plains, following the huge herds of buffalo that roamed there. The men hunted the buffalo using bows and arrows, originally on foot and later on horseback. The women prepared the skins for making into warm clothing and tepees. Tepees were the traditional homes of these nomadic tribes. They could be easily taken down and transported to the next site.

In winter the community would settle in one place in order to avoid the bitterly cold, harsh winters that occured on the plains. They would dry and store enough meat to last them the winter. Cooking was done over an open fire, often fuelled by dried buffalo dung, as there were so few trees to provide firewood.

Many of the traditional images we have of 'Indians' come from the peoples of the plains. Tepees are one image. Wearing the hair in two plaits is another, along with leggings and tunics made from deerskins. Some men wore head-dresses made from eagle feathers as a sign of their bravery in battle. The images of rain and war dances also come from the plains peoples.

One thing the people of the plains shared with other Native American peoples was a belief in a Great Spirit who influenced their lives. They also believed that many things in the natural world – sun, moon, wind, sky, water – had powerful influences and that animals, like humans, had spirits. Above all, they believed that no one could own the land. Chief Seathl of the Suquamish wrote a letter to the US government in which he explained their beliefs: 'The earth does not belong to man. Man belongs to the earth. This we know.'

Mountain Men

Following Lewis and Clark's expedition in 1804–1805, several men explored the area in and around the Rocky Mountains. Many of them lived alone, tracking and trapping animals for their fur, and living close to the Native American people. Often they lived in friendship with one another, but sometimes the Natives attacked the mountain men because they felt they were taking over their territory. The mountain men learned a great deal about how to hunt animals and to live in the harsh landscape of the Rockies.

These men were often a wild sight to see. They were frequently unshaven and long-haired, wearing deerskin trousers, beaver-skin hats and shirts decorated with leather fringes. Copying the native people, mountain men wore soft-soled moccasins that allowed them to creep up on prey without making a sound.

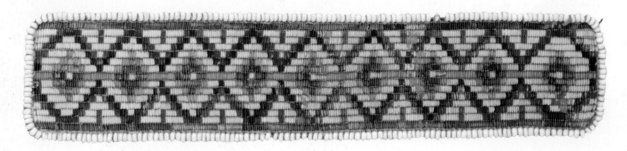

They also carried Indian weapons – such as small axes known as 'tomahawks' and skinning knives – as well as European pistols and rifles. Sometimes small animal skulls hung from their belts.

One of the most famous mountain men was Jim Bridger. He joined a fur-trapping expedition when he was about 18 years old. He found many routes through the Rockies, later escorting travellers to a new life in the West. Although he never learned to read, it was said he had a photographic memory for landscape, and that he used to create maps of the territory. He also learned French, and many Indian languages. In 1943 he built Fort Bridger, a staging post on the route to the West. Here people could rest in safety before continuing the long and dangerous journey westward.

Wagon Trains

Once people like Jim Bridger had established routes to the west coast and the lands of California and Oregon, the first settlers set out from the eastern United States. These people, called 'pioneers', were attracted by the idea of finding a new home or making their fortune.

From 1830 onwards, small groups of pioneers set off from towns in Missouri, like St Louis and Independence, to cross the Great Plains. In 1843 the first large group of pioneers left for Oregon. About 1,000 settlers made the difficult journey along the Oregon Trail. Whole families, including young babies and old people, travelled with all their belongings in covered wagons. The Great Plains were called the 'Prairie Ocean', so sometimes these wagons were referred to as 'prairie schooners' because they were like boats sailing on the grassland of the plains.

The Oregon Trail was dangerous. Progress was slow, usually less than 15 miles a day, and many people died on the way; 10,000 people died on the journey between 1835 and 1855. The pioneers faced attacks by Indians, outbreaks of diseases like cholera and smallpox, snow blizzards, and heavy rain that brought severe flooding.

Most of the people who made the journey to Oregon and California went there because they wanted a piece of land that they could farm themselves. Sometimes groups of them, like the Mormons, were escaping from religious persecution or from famine. Between 1845 and 1847 one and a half million people emigrated from Ireland because of famine. Thousands of them made their way to the west coast of America.

Gold Fever

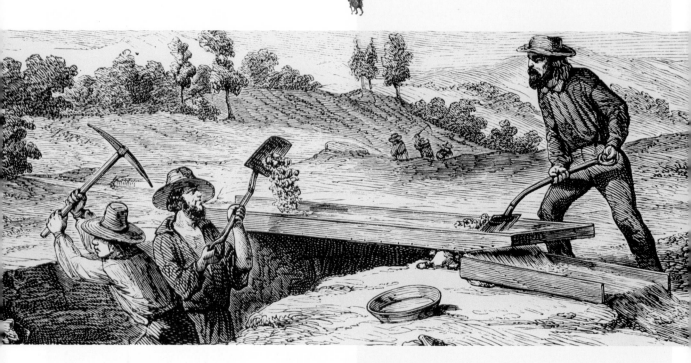

In 1848 gold was discovered in California. The following year most of the people making the journey West were very different from the families in their covered wagons. These were gold prospectors. They became known as the 'forty-niners' because this was the year the Californian Gold Rush started.

Much of the gold was found by 'panning'. The gold was washed out of the mountain rocks by streams. The gold then mixed with the gravel on the riverbed. Miners for gold took a pan, much like a frying pan, and filled it with river gravel and water. By swirling the pan around, the lighter material rose to the top. Gold is heavy so it sinks to the bottom and the panner searched the cleaned gravel for nuggets of gold.

Searching for gold was an uncomfortable business. The miners had to stand all day in the cold river water while the hot sun blazed down. Towns grew up around the areas where the panners worked. These were rough places with only wooden shacks and no proper roads. Often arguments would arise over who had the right to pan what area of river, and because there were very few law-men to keep the peace, fighting and shooting often broke out.

Although a few people did make a fortune, most did not, and it was the people like shopkeepers and blacksmiths, who came to provide for the miners' needs, that made the most money in the Californian Gold Rush.

Ranches on the Plains

The Great Plains, or prairies, were grasslands: thousands of miles of flat, open land. Throughout the 1830s, 40s and 50s most settlers had avoided the Plains, believing that they were no good for farming. However, during this time a number of herds of cattle grazed on the grasslands of Texas. Gradually, the frontier for grazing beef cattle moved north into the prairies of Kansas.

On the plains themselves, and in Texas, there was very little market for the beef. The main centres of population were in the east and on the west coast. In order to reach the markets, the cattle had to be driven there by cowboys.

Several people navigated trails north where they could pick up the newly-built railroads that ran from east to west. Jessie Chisholm blazed a trail from Texas to Kansas, and Charlie Goodnight and Oliver Loving made a trail to the Colorado gold mines to sell their beef to the miners.

In 1861 the American Civil War broke out. It lasted until 1865 and during that time there was a huge demand for beef to feed the armies on both sides. It became very profitable to raise beef and the number of cattle increased enormously.

People like Charlie Goodnight became very rich. They owned thousands of cattle, and by the 1880s the prairie had been divided up and fenced off into ranches. Instead of cattle roaming freely across the plains, they would graze on the huge ranches that covered thousands of hectares.

Cowboys

A cowboy's job was to look after the cattle on the ranch and on the trail. The work was very difficult and uncomfortable. There were dangers from Indians, rough weather and the cattle themselves, which could trample a cowboy to death in a stampede. Cowboys lived either in a 'bunkhouse' that they shared with all the other cowboys, or on the open plains. Either way they had very little privacy and few possessions.

Many of the things we associate with cowboys were related to their job. A horse was important in order to be able to follow the cattle. Most cowboys became very skilled on horseback, learning to rope cattle and round them up. The classic Stetson hat was important to shade them from the hot sun, but also made a good bowl for a man – or a horse – to drink water from. Cowboys wore 'chaps' (pronounced shaps), made from leather, over their denim jeans. These provided protection for their legs.

The guns or pistols that some cowboys carried were not really used in their work. A rifle was more likely to be used to kill a cow that was badly injured, or a wolf or cougar that threatened the herd.

When the cowboy went into town he might well take his gun. The cow towns that grew up along the cattle trails were, like the gold towns further west, rough and dangerous places. They were full of gambling dens and bars and often there was little law and order.

Homesteaders

In 1862, the US government passed a law that allowed any family to claim 65 hectares of land. If they farmed this land for five years, they could then claim it as their own. This 'Homestead Act' saw thousands of immigrants from Europe head west to the prairies to claim land. In their own countries they could never have hoped to own land. After the Civil War, when slavery was abolished, freed black slaves also claimed land on the prairies.

The Homestead Act had several consequences. The first was that the Native Americans were pushed off even more of the land that they had lived on freely for thousands of years. This loss of land had already begun with the growth in the number of ranches on the plains. The homesteaders also came into conflict with the ranch owners.

The ranch owners believed that the land belonged to them.

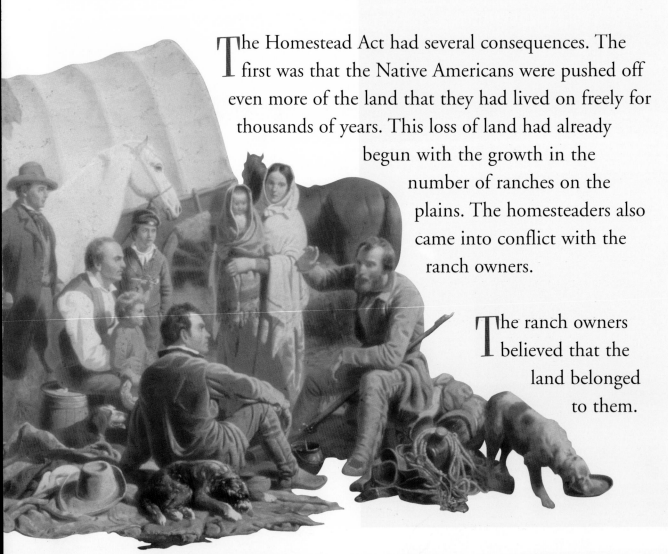

Disputes broke out between cowboys and the homesteaders, who were known as 'sodbusters' because they often built their homes from sods (or blocks) of earth as there were few trees on the plains to provide wood.

Like all pioneers, a homesteader's life was difficult. The prairie soil was hard to plough and difficult to cultivate. The area was prone to drought, heavy rain, thunderstorms, hailstones, winter blizzards and high winds. All of which threatened growing crops.

Despite the dangers and hardships, many homesteaders managed to claim their land and built thriving farms and communities. The arrival of homestead families also helped bring a more civilised lifestyle and law and order to the prairies.

The Pony Express

Settlers on the west coast of America were very isolated. News of national events could take weeks to reach California or Oregon, just as it took nearly six months for news of the Californian gold find to reach the east. Getting personal news or letters from friends or relatives was even more difficult. There were mail services set up, but they could take weeks or months.

In April 1860 a new mail service began. This was the Pony Express and guaranteed to get the mail from St Joseph in Missouri in just ten days.

The Pony Express was the idea of William Russell. He hired 80 of the best riders, and bought 500 of the fastest ponies. Stations where horses could be changed were placed at 15-mile intervals along the length of the 2,000 mile route.

The mail was carried in a *mochila*, a sheet of leather with four locked leather pouches, one at each corner. The *mochila* fitted over the saddle and the rider sat on it. It could be quickly transferred from one pony to the next. Each rider travelled about 75 miles a day at full gallop, changing ponies every 15 miles. The mail had to cover 200 miles every day.

The Pony Express lasted only 18 months. In October 1861 a telegraph line to California was established. News and messages could cross the continent in seconds rather than days or weeks. However, the bravery of the Pony Express riders in the face of attack by Indians, outlaws and terrible weather, and the fact that only one of the thousands of deliveries was ever lost, made it a legend of the Wild West.

The Railroad

Stage coach companies were set up to transport people, mail and gold across America. However, the journey across the plains and the Rockies was a very uncomfortable and slow one. It was dangerous too. Stage coaches could not travel very fast, and were targets for outlaws and Native Americans who were beginning to rebel at the invasion of their lands.

A railway, or railroad, was the answer to many of the transport problems between the east and the west. From the 1850s onwards, the US government encouraged railroad companies to build rail lines across the country.

The railway companies were given large amounts of land by the government. They built their lines and then sold the land on to settlers, who were transported to the area by the railroad.

Building the railroad across America was a great feat of engineering, as well as very hard work for the labourers who worked on it. There was no heavy machinery to make the work easier; digging, lifting and carrying were done by hand, with horses to help. Workers were sometimes attacked by Native Americans, who were determined to stop the railroad. Thousands of workers were brought in from China by the Central Pacific company, who were building the line eastward from California.

In May 1869, at a place called Promontory in Utah, the line built by Central Pacific joined the line being built westward by the Union Pacific company – the East and West Coasts of America were united.

Ghost Towns

Ghost towns exist all over America. Most are old mining towns. The only reason for their existence was to supply the needs of the miners who worked there. When the minerals ran out, the miners left and so did everyone else.

It was not only gold that people searched for in the west of America. Silver, copper and other minerals were also sought after. However, in the Wild West it was chiefly gold and silver.

Virginia City, Nevada, is now a ghost town and a great tourist attraction. In 1859, the Comstock Lode, a rich deposit of gold and silver was found near here. In 1875, Virginia City had a population of 20,000, and when it was burnt down in a fire, it was rebuilt. Despite its size and the efforts that had gone into rebuilding it, by 1890 most of the population had left because the minerals had run out.

One of the most famous ghost towns is Tombstone, Arizona. It too is now a popular tourist attraction. Visitors come to see the Boot Hill Cemetery, where many of the Wild West's most well-known outlaws are buried. They also visit the OK Corral, where a famous gun battle took place in 1881, between the Clanton family and Marshall Wyatt Earp, his brothers and Doc Holliday.

Justice in the Wild West

In many areas, especially mining areas, towns grew rapidly – within just a few years there could be a community of several thousand people, mostly men without wives and families. Their only occupations when not working were drinking and gambling. Often fights broke out, and as many people wore guns, there was sometimes shooting.

There were also people who planned and carried out robberies and other crimes. In the mining towns, miners were robbed of their gold or silver. Cattle 'rustling', or poaching, was another common crime. Some of the more daring criminals, like Jesse James and his gang, held up the stage coaches and, later, the trains that transported gold or money; others held up banks in small towns.

Towns would employ a sheriff or marshal, who would try to keep law and order, locking up the drunks and petty criminals. The town blacksmith would usually make a large iron cage that served as a gaol.

People accused of crimes would be tried by a judge who travelled around a particular area, holding court in each town. Often people were hanged for their crimes.

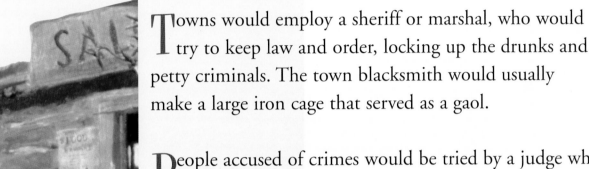

However, very often justice was not so straightforward. In areas where there were no sheriffs, marshals or judges, the local townspeople would take it upon themselves to try and sentence those they believed had committed crimes. The 'criminals' were usually hanged. Sometimes there would be no trial at all; the criminals were 'lynched' – that is, they were hunted down and hanged from the nearest tree.

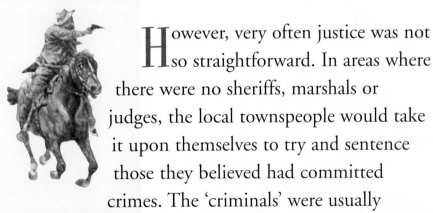

War Between the Settlers and the Native Americans

When Europeans first came to America they were welcomed by the Native American peoples, who taught them much about the land, its animals, its plants and how to survive.

Most of the settlers felt themselves to be superior to what they saw as the 'savage and uncivilised' native peoples, and were unconcerned when millions of them died from European diseases. In 1838 President Jackson decided that the Cherokee people could no longer stay in their home state of Georgia. Like many other Native Americans before them, they were forced to leave their land and made to travel thousands of miles to land the white settlers did not want.

The Native American peoples of the Plains suffered the same fate. At first, in 1851, the US government agreed that the Native Americans could have a large area of land in return for some of it being given to settlers. However, this promise did not last, and in 1861 some braves of the Cheyenne tribe went on the warpath to protest at the invasion of their lands in Colorado, particularly by gold prospectors.

In response to this, American soldiers massacred every man, woman and child in a Cheyenne village called Sand Creek. It was the start of a war between the US government and settlers and the Native American peoples of the plains that lasted for 30 years.

The Battle of Wounded Knee

Not only had the settlers taken the native peoples' land, but they were responsible for the rapid disappearance of the buffalo. Millions of buffalo were shot by the settlers for their hides or for meat. They were also kept from their grazing land by the fencing-in of the prairies and many were shot needlessly for sport, their carcasses left to rot on the plains. William Cody earned his nickname 'Buffalo Bill' from shooting buffalo. This was very bad for the Native Americans, who needed the buffalo to survive.

The US government sent soldiers to try to protect the settlers from attack. These soldiers were stationed in fortified barracks like Fort Laramie. Native American Chiefs such as Sitting Bull, Red Cloud and Black Kettle, led their braves in major battles against the US army. Their greatest victory was in 1876 at the Battle of the Little Bighorn. Sioux and Cheyenne braves killed 210 US soldiers, including their leader General Custer.

After this, the government were determined to defeat the Native Americans. Many of the Chiefs were captured and their people moved to Reservations – special areas where the government could control them.

In 1889 a new religion started among the Native Americans. The religion was based on the 'Ghost Dance', in which the spirits of dead ancestors were called upon to help defeat the white settlers. The soldiers were called in to stop the Indians from practising this religion and in the fight, Chief Sitting Bull was was killed. Sitting Bull's followers were pursued by US cavalry who caught up with them at a Sioux village called Wounded Knee, where more than 150 Native American men, women and children were killed.

It was the last major battle in the war. The settlers had won and the Native Americans were forced to live on the Reservations.

Wild West Shows

As well as being a rider on the Pony Express, William Cody was also a scout for the US Army, a fighter of Native Americans and a cowboy. He also worked as an actor on Broadway, New York. He is better known as Buffalo Bill, a nickname he earned when he was employed by a railroad company to shoot buffalo to supply meat for the workers.

During the 1870s, he became famous as the hero of numerous cowboy stories published in cheap 'dime' novels. He also spent much of this time as a showman, giving demonstrations of cowboy skills. Sometimes he worked with Wild Bill Hickok, who was later shot dead while playing poker in the town of Deadwood.

In 1882 Buffalo Bill organised a series of events in his home town of North Platte, Nebraska, to celebrate Independence Day. The events included shooting, riding, working with a lasso and other cowboy skills. The event was so popular that Cody decided to take it on the road.

The Wild West Show developed and travelled across America, and finally to Europe. In 1887 Buffalo Bill and his fellow show people performed in London for Queen Victoria.

Annie Oakley performed with Buffalo Bill. She was a crack shot. Even before joining the Wild West Show she was famous as a professional game hunter.

The Wild West Show, along with the popular 'dime' novels, did much to spread the image we have today of the cowboy and the Native American.

Further Information

Places to Visit

British Museum – Great Russell Street, London, WC1B 3DG.
Telephone: 0171 636 1555.
Horniman Museum – 100 London Road, Forest Hill, London, SE23 3PQ.
Telephone: 0181 699 1872.

Further Reading

Children on the Oregon Trail by A Rutgers Van der Loeff – an adventure story of a group of children trying to make the journey west.

The Little House on the Prairie by Laura Ingles Wilder – the story of a family of settlers trying to survive on the Plains.

The Last of the Mohicans by James Fennimore Cooper – this book was also made in to a film in 1990. It is not about the West but its main character is a white frontiersman between the settlers in the east and his admiration of the Native Americans. It was written in 1826 so is a challenging read.

Shane by Jack Schaeffer – the story of a young boy on a homestead who makes friend with a mysterious stranger who helps in the battle against the local ranch owner. This book has also been made into a film of the same name.

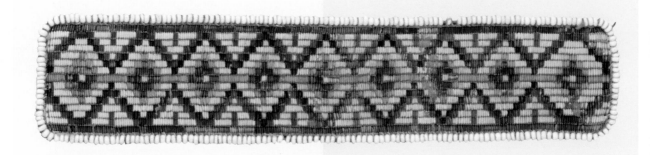

Videos and Films

Broken Arrow – the first film to show things from the perspective of the Native American people.

Butch Cassidy and the Sundance Kid – an account of the lives of two of the West's outlaws. Although they are portrayed as nicer than they probably were, it is reasonably accurate.

Dances with Wolves – a US cavalry man sent to an outpost makes friends with and comes to understand the Native Americans.

High Noon – a classic western, with the sheriff facing a shoot-out with the outlaws at noon.

Red River – following the cattle trail to Kansas

She Wore a Yellow Ribbon – a story set with the US Cavalry in the West.

Stagecoach – the story of a set of travellers' adventures as they cross America.

The Big Country – an easterner travels west to marry a ranch owner's daughter. He learns about the way of life of many of the different types of settler – ranch owners, cowboys, homesteaders.

Picture Credits